Our Gay Wedding Day

Our Gay Wedding Day
William Giancursio

wgiancursio@prodigy.net
ISBN: 978-0-6152-4470-9

Prelude

As an artist who is also gay, it is often difficult to separate my identity from my work. I am willing to take chances with the issues that I portray as I am not afraid of labels anymore. The prevailing attitude is one of internalized homophobia. This attitude is not only held by straight society, but also by many gay men and women, particularly those who have achieved certain levels of success. It is frequently directed at aspects of gay culture and behavior which are considered inappropriate by society. In my case finding suitable venues for my art work has proven to be particularly arduous. The point of view I have encountered is that it is ok for me to be a gay artist, as long as my art isn't too gay. Or as one gallery owner once said to me, "In New York City, we're over the gay issue," as if gay culture had been suddenly homogenized into the mainstream of society and we all lived in an egalitarian world. Prevailing hatred and intolerance toward cultural minorities speak to the contrary. People are just getting better at concealing their disdain toward one another. As we move into the 21st century, I can not believe that legislation which would ensure equality under the law for gay, lesbian, bisexual, and transgender people lags far behind the "liberated" times many others believe we live in.

In addition to being a freelance artist, I am also an adjunct faculty member at a highly regarded university here in upstate New York, where I have taught drawing and design for the past 20 years. Even so, I once had a series of my photographs removed from an exhibit on campus. They were taken down because one of the employees who worked in the office where they were exhibited was uncomfortable with the gay narrative and felt that the photographs were inappropriate. Not quite what one would expect from an institute of higher learning, or so I thought.

Homophobia is alive and well everywhere! Artists have faced opposition and censorship for centuries at the whims of the ignorant, narrow-minded and uninformed, yet freedom of expression prevails, which is the best reason I know to persevere. Times are in fact changing, although not fast enough for many of us. The role of the artist to educate and facilitate change has never been silenced for very long and artists have always been foremost in changing attitudes and reshaping public opinion. To inform, communicate and enlighten is what my art is all about.

In a greater sense, my work celebrates gay culture and diversity. The picture I portray isn't always agreeable to everyone. In this regard my photos can be viewed as confrontational. They challenge by presenting issues and exploring individual comfort levels. Objectively they portray segments of gay culture which do in fact exist regardless of whether the viewer understands or agrees. My work is also subjective in that it represents my point of view. Yet I believe that the intrinsic nature of art is neutral. Art is a catalyst which speaks to us on many levels. These levels are variable depending on the unique understanding or lack thereof on the part of the viewer. This "truth" to me is absolute, so in the best sense, what one brings to the experience of viewing art, as in all things, determines what one will come away with.

At its best my art is ambiguous and ironic, because in every photograph lies the co-existence of truth and falsehood. My photographs also reflect a central truth about the lives of gay men; things are not only as they appear to be, but they also appear to be other than what they are.

When I was growing up if boys played with dolls they were considered sissies. So I built model cars and played with guns and toy soldiers until I became totally bored. Eventually I staged mock wars and multi-car pile-ups and (with the aid of lighter fluid) torched my toys in frustration and secretly longed for more creative outlets (I also ran out of toys). I envied my girl cousins because of the wide range of play they had available to them in the form of dolls, little people, friends who presented them with endless hours of play scenarios. I, on the other hand, could only wage a war or build a model car.

In 1959 Mattel introduced the 11" fashion doll. By then I was too old to play with toys; besides I wasn't quite as interested in playing with Barbie as I was with her boyfriend Ken. When Hasbro designed GI Joe in 1964 I really felt cheated. Here, at last, was a "doll" made for boys to play with, and he came with a multitude of accessories and accoutrements too. Finally, society gave its stamp of approval for boys to play with dolls (rather, action figures), but I was almost old enough to fight in a real war.

In 1966 in the midst of the Vietnam War I was drafted. I still have a photo of my four-year-old godson Julius, standing at attention, dressed in a pretend army uniform, with two GI Joe action figures on either side of him. All three of them are saluting me. It sat above my bunk for two years. In 1966 a boy's play options were still limited to acts of war. Grown men today, it seems, still have a socialized proclivity toward aggression and war.

Ten years later my studies of art and film in college were impacted by viewing a remarkable award-winning film produced by the Canadian film board entitled "Toys." In the film a group of children are seen looking through a toy store window at Christmastime. They soon become witness to the horrors of war when a huge display of military toys comes to life and they go to war with each other. The brutal 3D animation scenes occur amid close-up still images of the children's smiling faces. The animation was incredibly lifelike, the message profound.

In the mid 1970's, thanks primarily to the feminist movement, the concept of sexism and the manner in which children are indoctrinated made many of us question the nature of play, and the toys which define play. Feminism made us think twice about the trucks and war toys we gave to little boys that strengthened masculine stereotypes of aggression and the baby-dolls which instilled maternal behavior in little girls. And then there was the 11" fashion doll, who established a new proportionally impossible standard of feminine beauty. In "Barbie's Queer Accessories," Erica Rand devotes an entire book to the politics of Barbie, including Barbie's origination from a German doll named Lilli who had been marketed primarily for adults. As children, life was so enchanting in our imaginary world of playful escapism. I think there is great "play" appeal for adults who purchase fashion dolls, action figures, and all of their accessories. What better way to secretly embrace childhood once again?

Today, I am a gay child reborn, playing with action figures and dolls in much the same way that children mimic adult life through play, only my play is gay-oriented. My conclusion is that although fashion dolls and action figures are designed and destined to reinforce heterosexual role-play, at least 10% of us (according to Kinsey's report on the occurrence of homosexuality in society) actually reinforce gay role-play, evidenced by the children playing with them who ultimately grow up to be gay.

Prelude

As an artist who is also gay, it is often difficult to separate my identity from my work. I am willing to take chances with the issues that I portray as I am not afraid of labels anymore. The prevailing attitude is one of internalized homophobia. This attitude is not only held by straight society, but also by many gay men and women, particularly those who have achieved certain levels of success. It is frequently directed at aspects of gay culture and behavior which are considered inappropriate by society. In my case finding suitable venues for my art work has proven to be particularly arduous. The point of view I have encountered is that it is ok for me to be a gay artist, as long as my art isn't too gay. Or as one gallery owner once said to me, "In New York City, we're over the gay issue," as if gay culture had been suddenly homogenized into the mainstream of society and we all lived in an egalitarian world. Prevailing hatred and intolerance toward cultural minorities speak to the contrary. People are just getting better at concealing their disdain toward one another. As we move into the 21st century, I can not believe that legislation which would ensure equality under the law for gay, lesbian, bisexual, and transgender people lags far behind the "liberated" times many others believe we live in.

In addition to being a freelance artist, I am also an adjunct faculty member at a highly regarded university here in upstate New York, where I have taught drawing and design for the past 20 years. Even so, I once had a series of my photographs removed from an exhibit on campus. They were taken down because one of the employees who worked in the office where they were exhibited was uncomfortable with the gay narrative and felt that the photographs were inappropriate. Not quite what one would expect from an institute of higher learning, or so I thought.

Homophobia is alive and well everywhere! Artists have faced opposition and censorship for centuries at the whims of the ignorant, narrow-minded and uninformed, yet freedom of expression prevails, which is the best reason I know to persevere. Times are in fact changing, although not fast enough for many of us. The role of the artist to educate and facilitate change has never been silenced for very long and artists have always been foremost in changing attitudes and reshaping public opinion. To inform, communicate and enlighten is what my art is all about.

In a greater sense, my work celebrates gay culture and diversity. The picture I portray isn't always agreeable to everyone. In this regard my photos can be viewed as confrontational. They challenge by presenting issues and exploring individual comfort levels. Objectively they portray segments of gay culture which do in fact exist regardless of whether the viewer understands or agrees. My work is also subjective in that it represents my point of view. Yet I believe that the intrinsic nature of art is neutral. Art is a catalyst which speaks to us on many levels. These levels are variable depending on the unique understanding or lack thereof on the part of the viewer. This "truth" to me is absolute, so in the best sense, what one brings to the experience of viewing art, as in all things, determines what one will come away with.

At its best my art is ambiguous and ironic, because in every photograph lies the co-existence of truth and falsehood. My photographs also reflect a central truth about the lives of gay men; things are not only as they appear to be, but they also appear to be other than what they are.

When I was growing up if boys played with dolls they were considered sissies. So I built model cars and played with guns and toy soldiers until I became totally bored. Eventually I staged mock wars and multi-car pile-ups and (with the aid of lighter fluid) torched my toys in frustration and secretly longed for more creative outlets (I also ran out of toys). I envied my girl cousins because of the wide range of play they had available to them in the form of dolls, little people, friends who presented them with endless hours of play scenarios. I, on the other hand, could only wage a war or build a model car.

In 1959 Mattel introduced the 11" fashion doll. By then I was too old to play with toys; besides I wasn't quite as interested in playing with Barbie as I was with her boyfriend Ken. When Hasbro designed GI Joe in 1964 I really felt cheated. Here, at last, was a "doll" made for boys to play with, and he came with a multitude of accessories and accoutrements too. Finally, society gave its stamp of approval for boys to play with dolls (rather, action figures), but I was almost old enough to fight in a real war.

In 1966 in the midst of the Vietnam War I was drafted. I still have a photo of my four-year-old godson Julius, standing at attention, dressed in a pretend army uniform, with two GI Joe action figures on either side of him. All three of them are saluting me. It sat above my bunk for two years. In 1966 a boy's play options were still limited to acts of war. Grown men today, it seems, still have a socialized proclivity toward aggression and war.

Ten years later my studies of art and film in college were impacted by viewing a remarkable award-winning film produced by the Canadian film board entitled "Toys." In the film a group of children are seen looking through a toy store window at Christmastime. They soon become witness to the horrors of war when a huge display of military toys comes to life and they go to war with each other. The brutal 3D animation scenes occur amid close-up still images of the children's smiling faces. The animation was incredibly lifelike, the message profound.

In the mid 1970's, thanks primarily to the feminist movement, the concept of sexism and the manner in which children are indoctrinated made many of us question the nature of play, and the toys which define play. Feminism made us think twice about the trucks and war toys we gave to little boys that strengthened masculine stereotypes of aggression and the baby-dolls which instilled maternal behavior in little girls. And then there was the 11" fashion doll, who established a new proportionally impossible standard of feminine beauty. In "Barbie's Queer Accessories," Erica Rand devotes an entire book to the politics of Barbie, including Barbie's origination from a German doll named Lilli who had been marketed primarily for adults. As children, life was so enchanting in our imaginary world of playful escapism. I think there is great "play" appeal for adults who purchase fashion dolls, action figures, and all of their accessories. What better way to secretly embrace childhood once again?

Today, I am a gay child reborn, playing with action figures and dolls in much the same way that children mimic adult life through play, only my play is gay-oriented. My conclusion is that although fashion dolls and action figures are designed and destined to reinforce heterosexual role-play, at least 10% of us (according to Kinsey's report on the occurrence of homosexuality in society) actually reinforce gay role-play, evidenced by the children playing with them who ultimately grow up to be gay.

My work is play, but it is conceptually about the nature of gay play. It is a serious and lyrical look at who we are, what we do, and some of our aspirations. My exploration is not at all about portraying these dolls and action figures in a subversive manner or a negative context. It is more about recognizing and validating these toys as also part of the childhood of every child who grew up to be gay. It is a visual journal of gay culture and the natural order of things from a gay perspective: boys with boys, and girls with girls. Who the toys represent is not my agenda, what they represent is. Because I am not ashamed of my gay orientation, I take pride in portraying the culture it represents through my artwork.

"Our Gay Wedding Day" is the first of what I hope will be a series of books that focus on the nature of gay play. The amount of time I spent building sets, making props and costumes, and of course photographing the events, is beyond measure. This wedding album represents what I consider to be the best and most essential results of sorting through over 1,200 digital photographs that took an entire year to stage and shoot. It chronicles the special day in the life of a fictitious gay couple who decide to get married. I wanted to follow them through the entire day from waking up in the morning until the conclusion of their wedding reception. How cool/absurd is that? Just remember as you view these photographs that what you bring to the experience will determine what you will come away with.

You are cordially invited to attend "Our Gay Wedding Day". Sit back, drink a toast, have a piece of cake, but most of all open your mind and enjoy the experience.

Events

Once Upon A Time

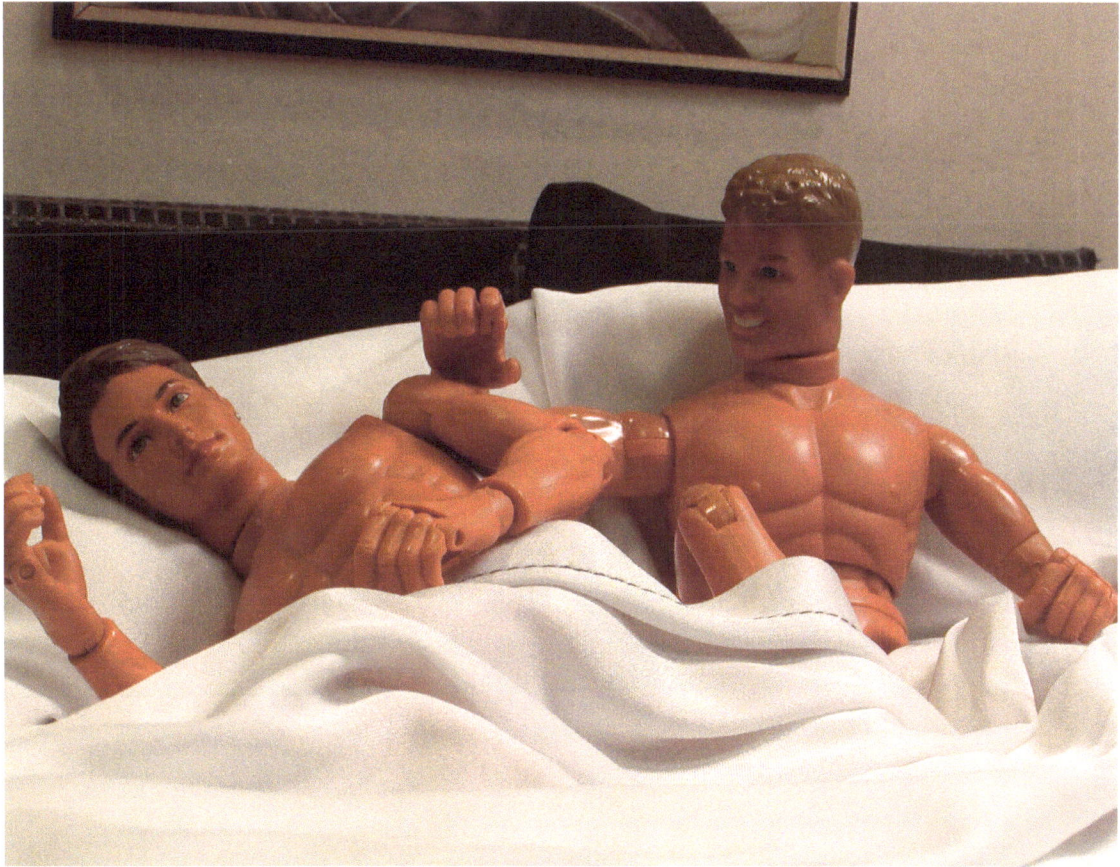

Pillow Fight

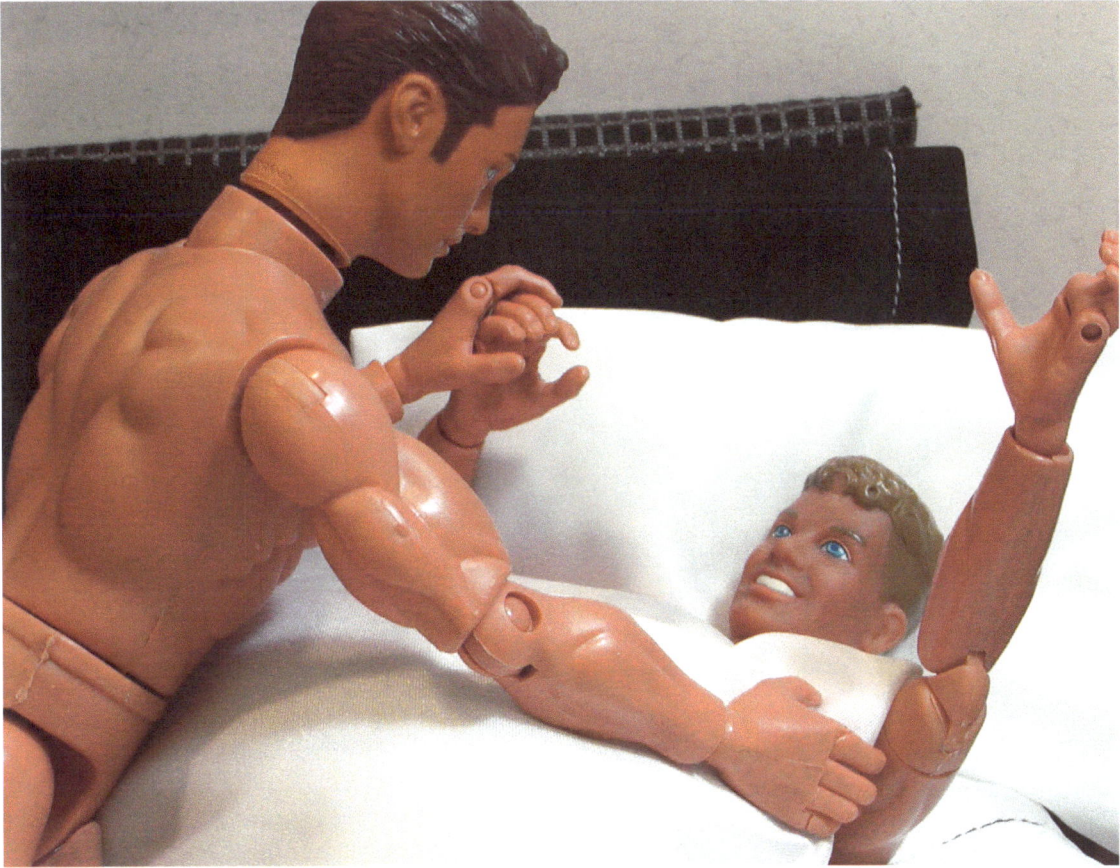
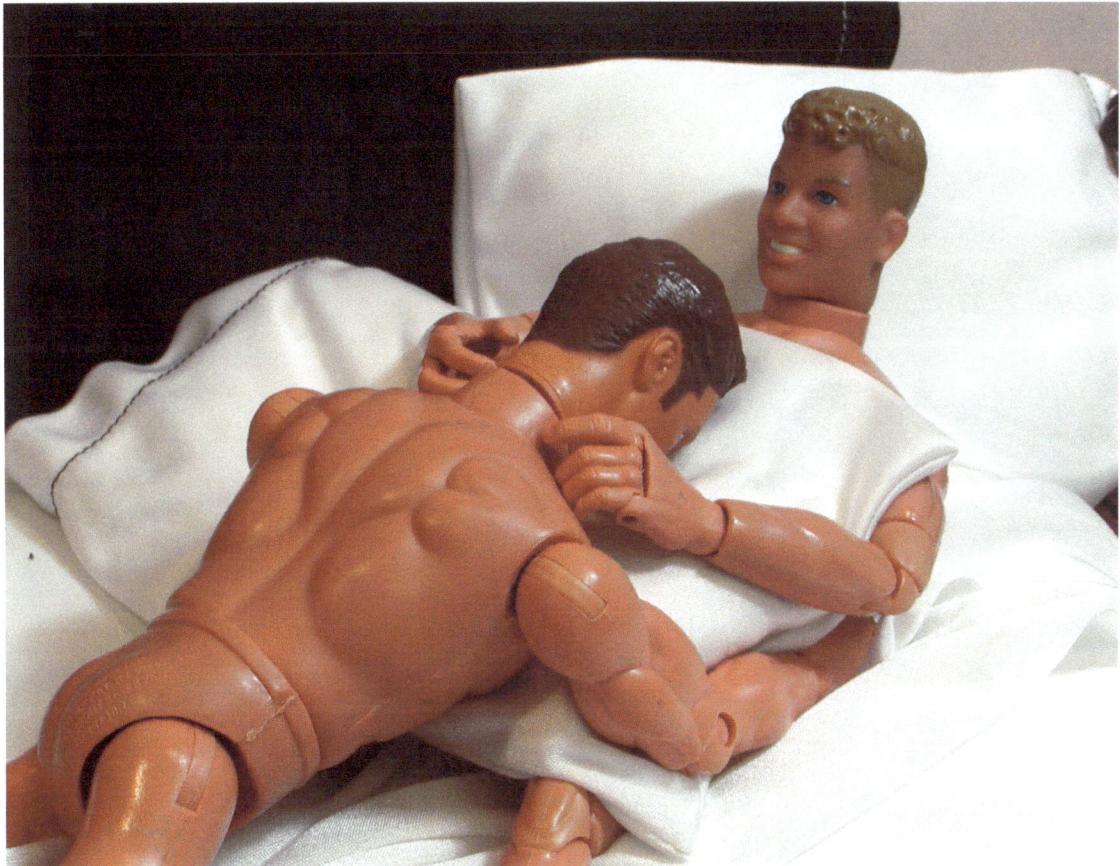

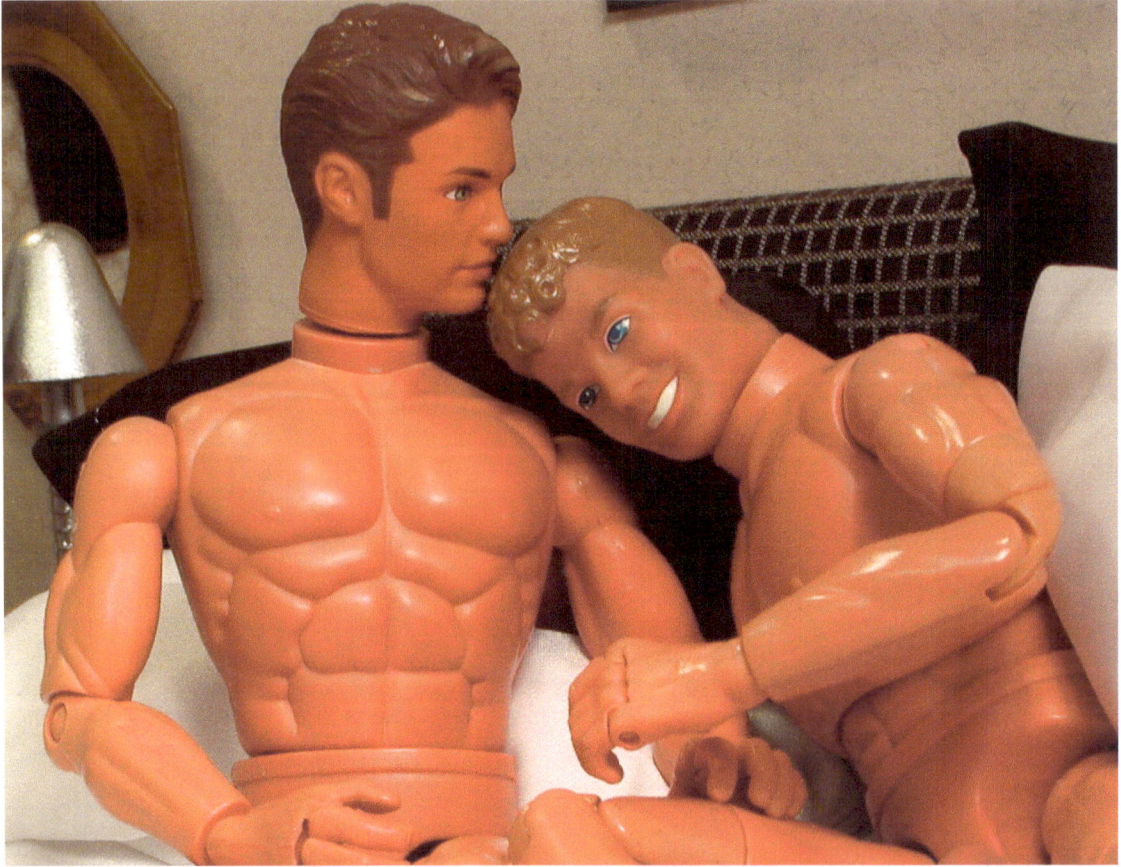

Breakfast Time

The Groomsmen Arrive

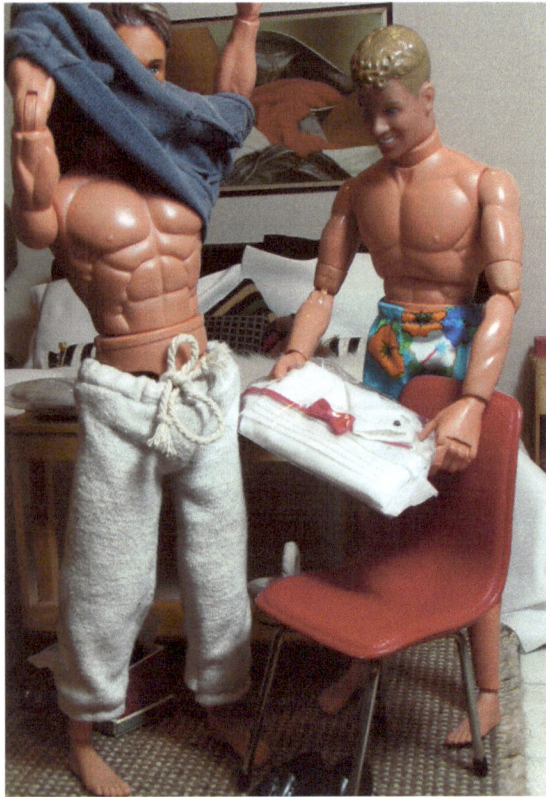
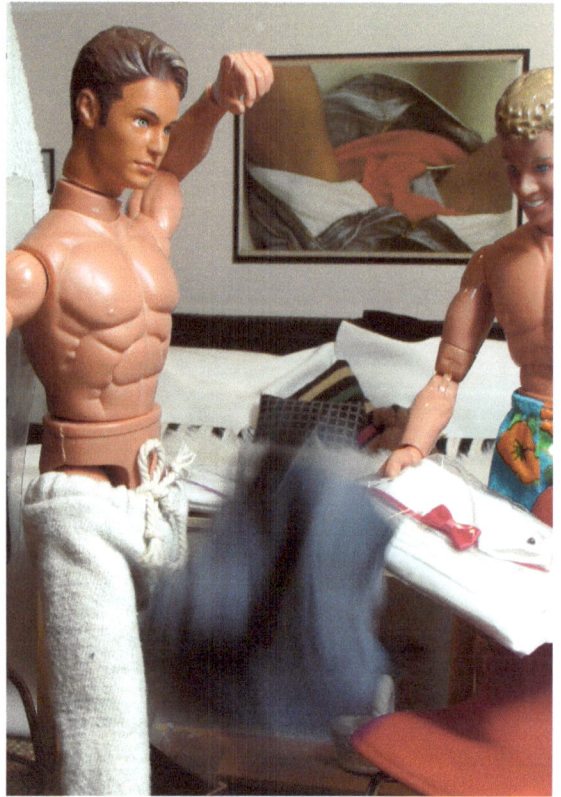

Looking Grand

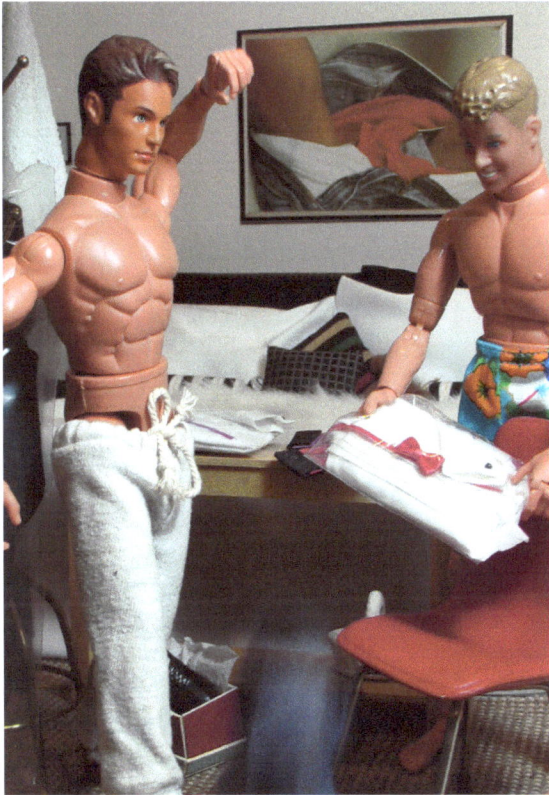
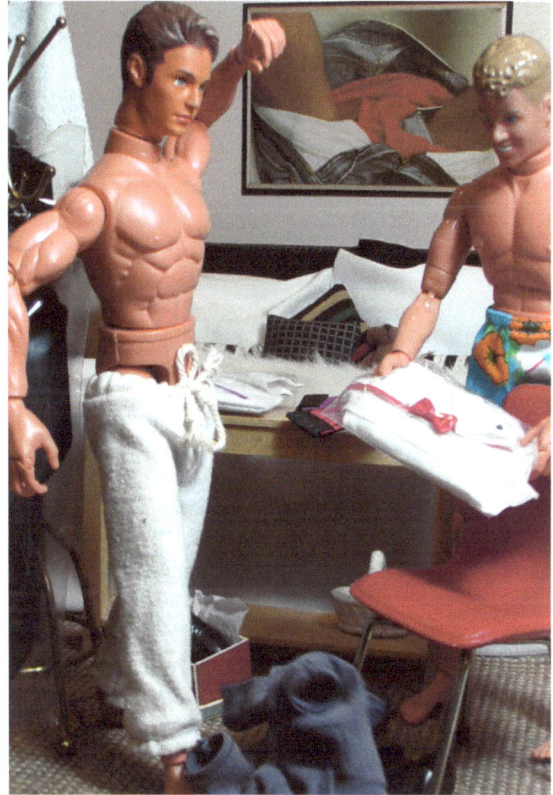

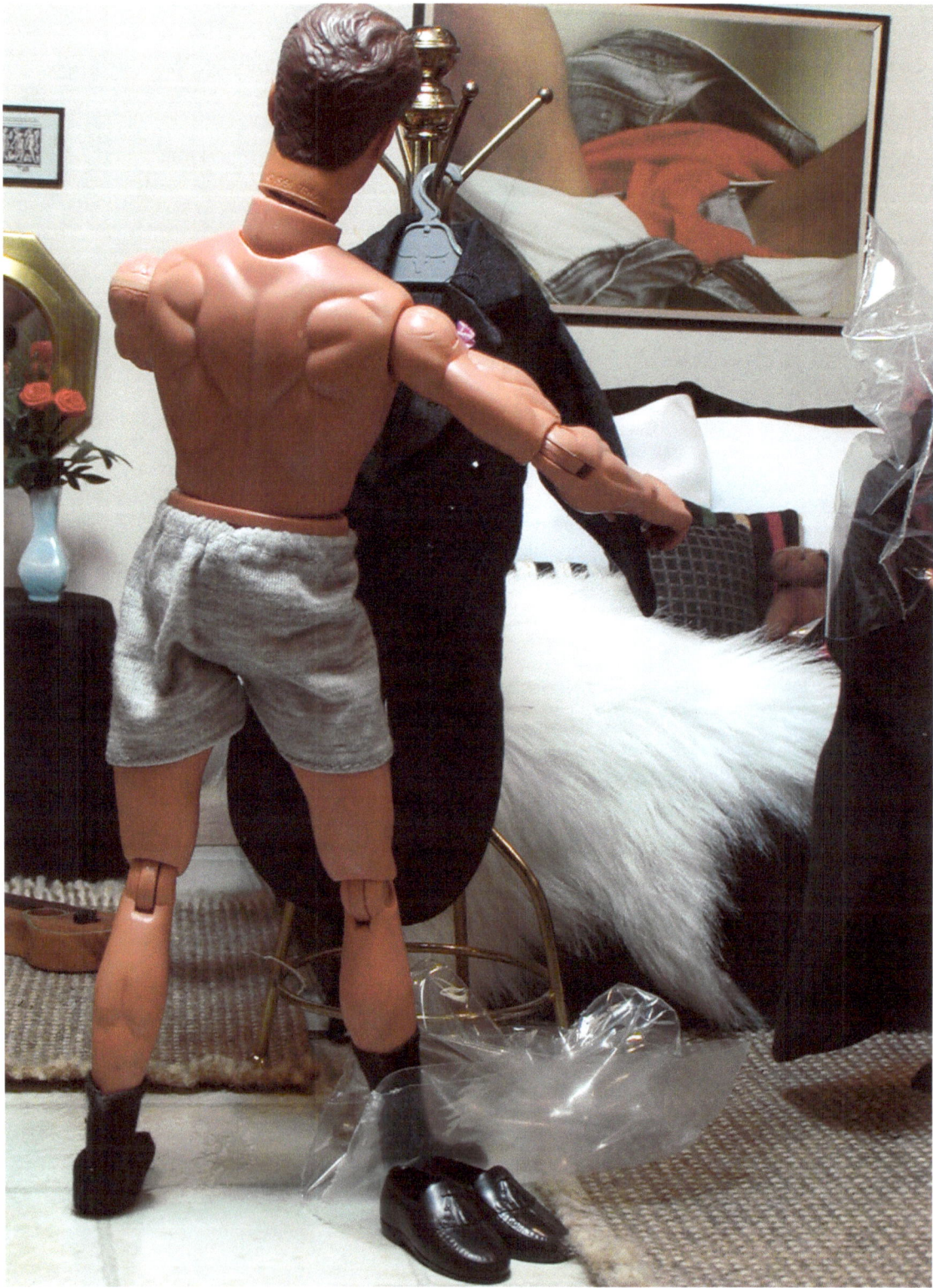

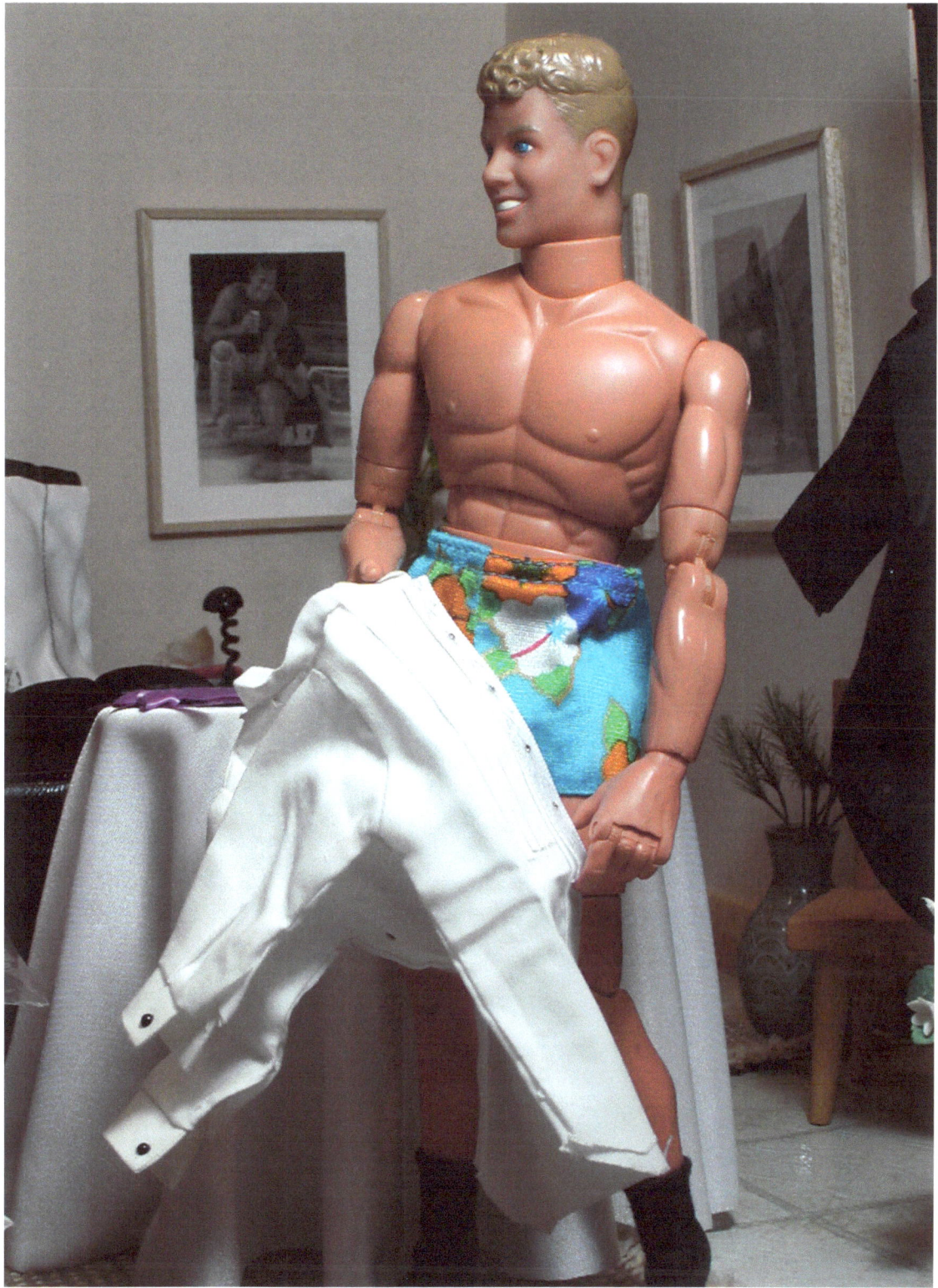

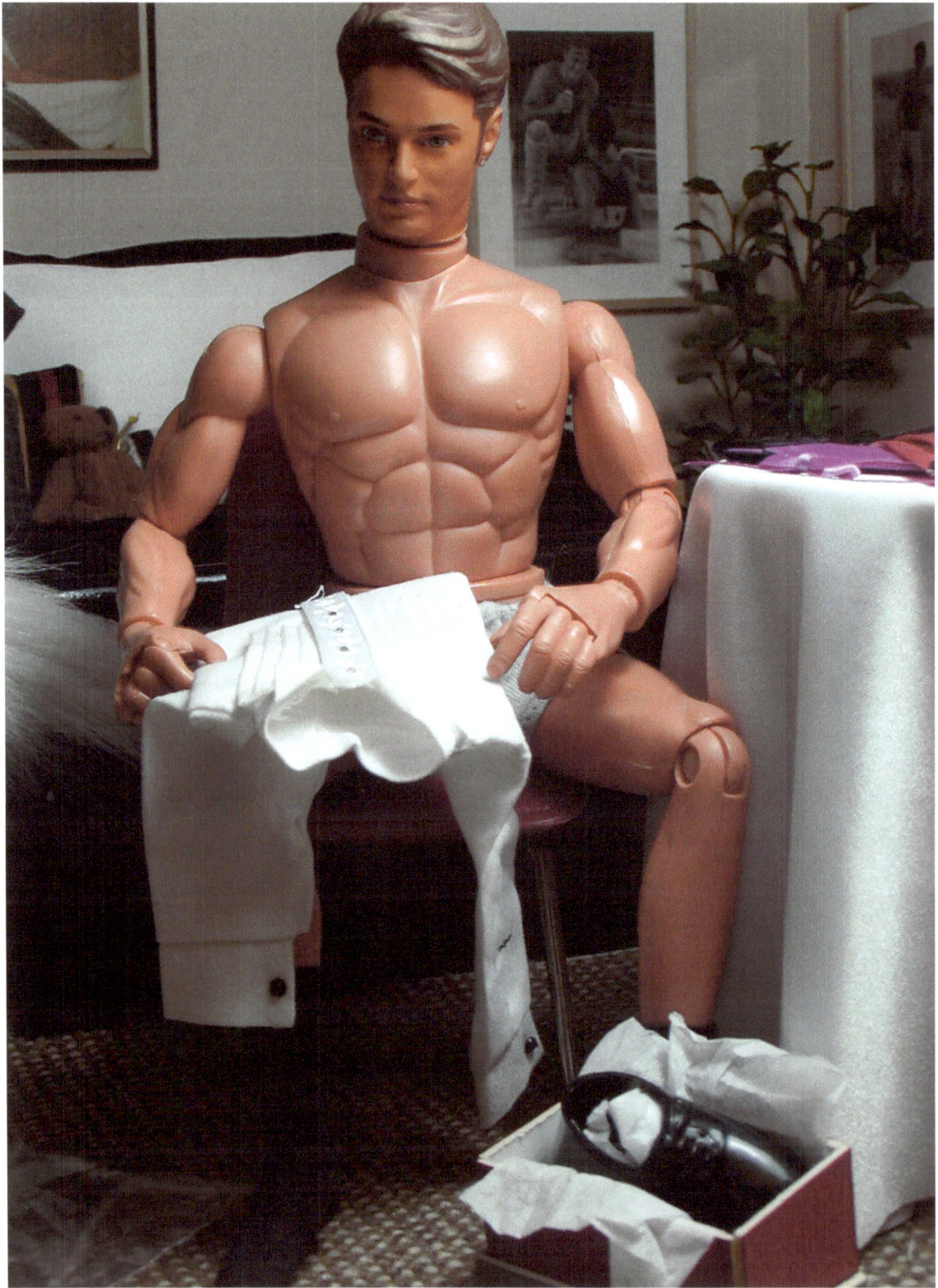

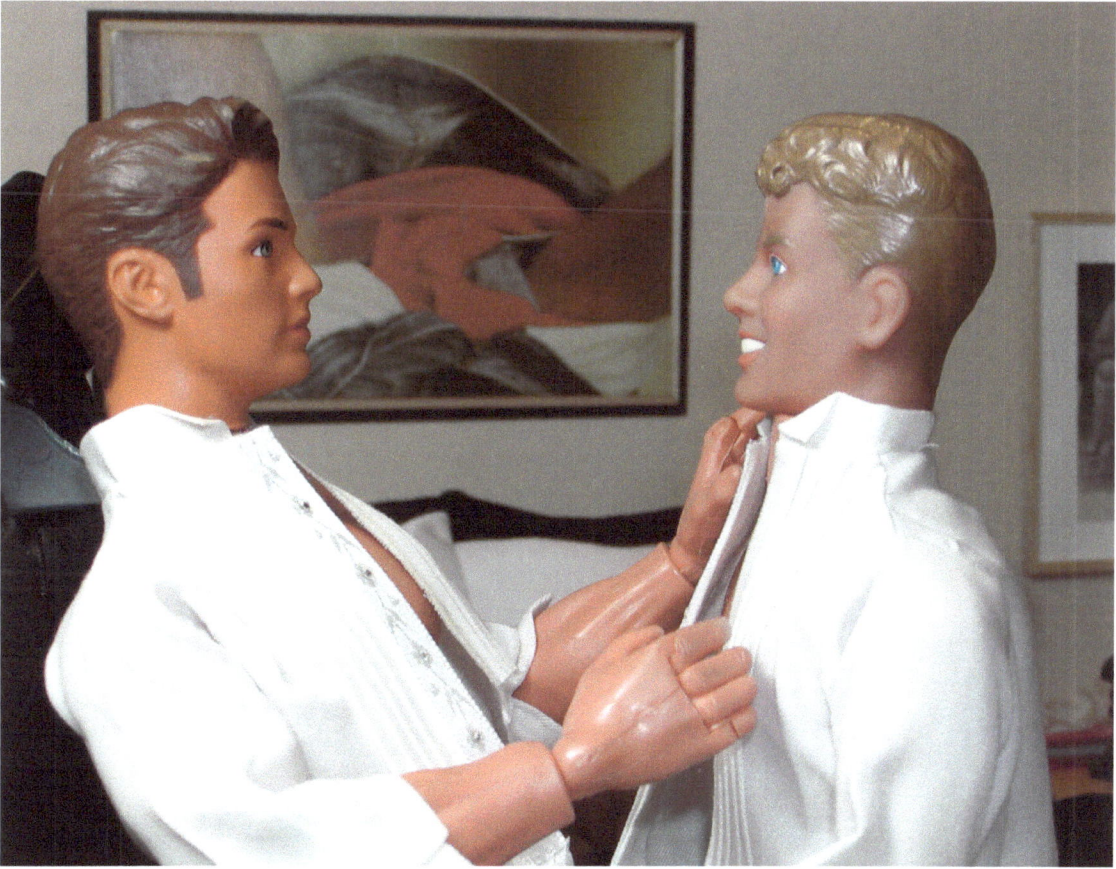

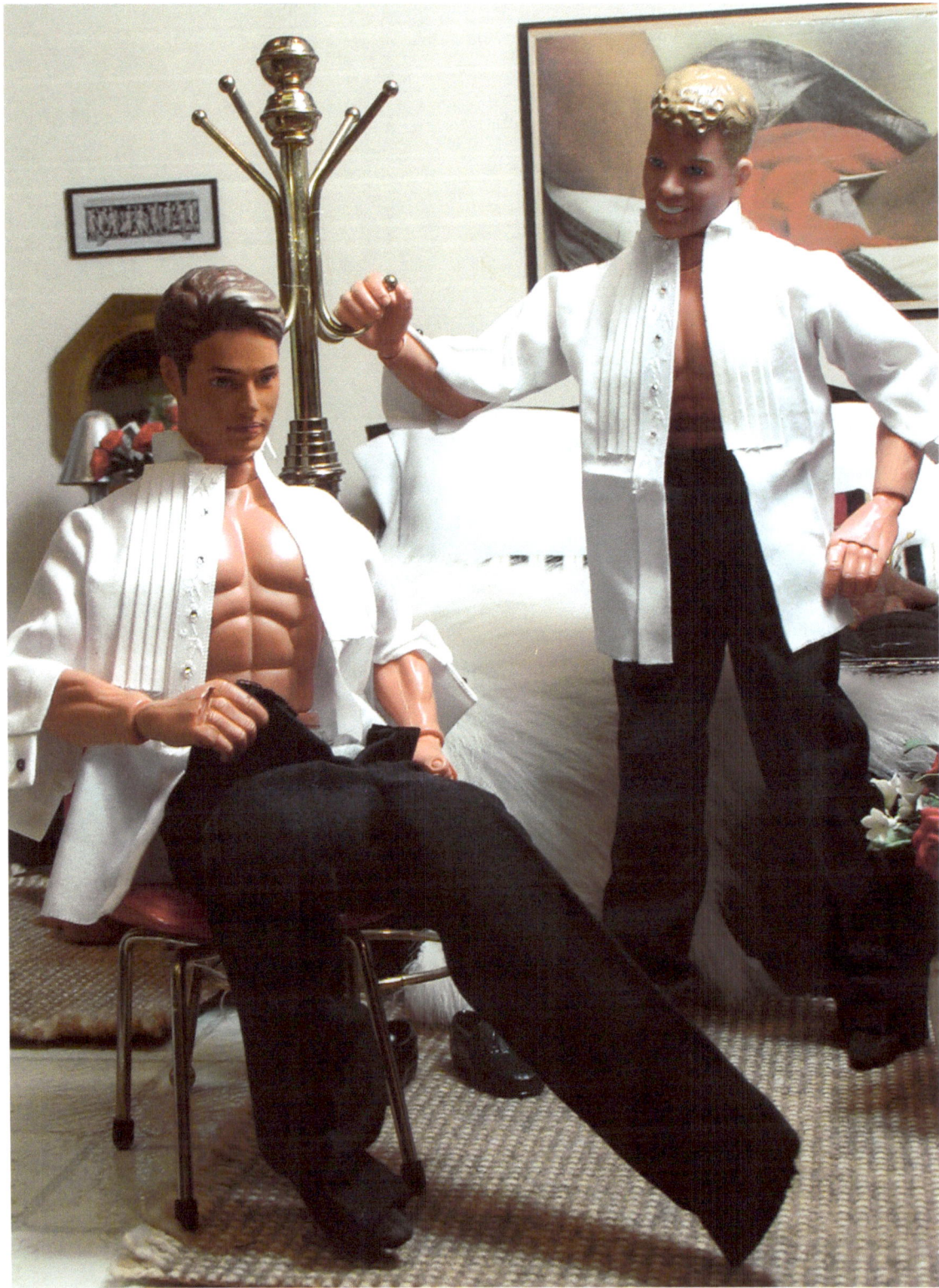

Family Pictures

Here's To Us

Back to the Garden

Dearly Beloved

Champagne!

71

Toasting the Grooms

Eat, Drink and be Merry

Having Our Cake...

May I Have this Dance?

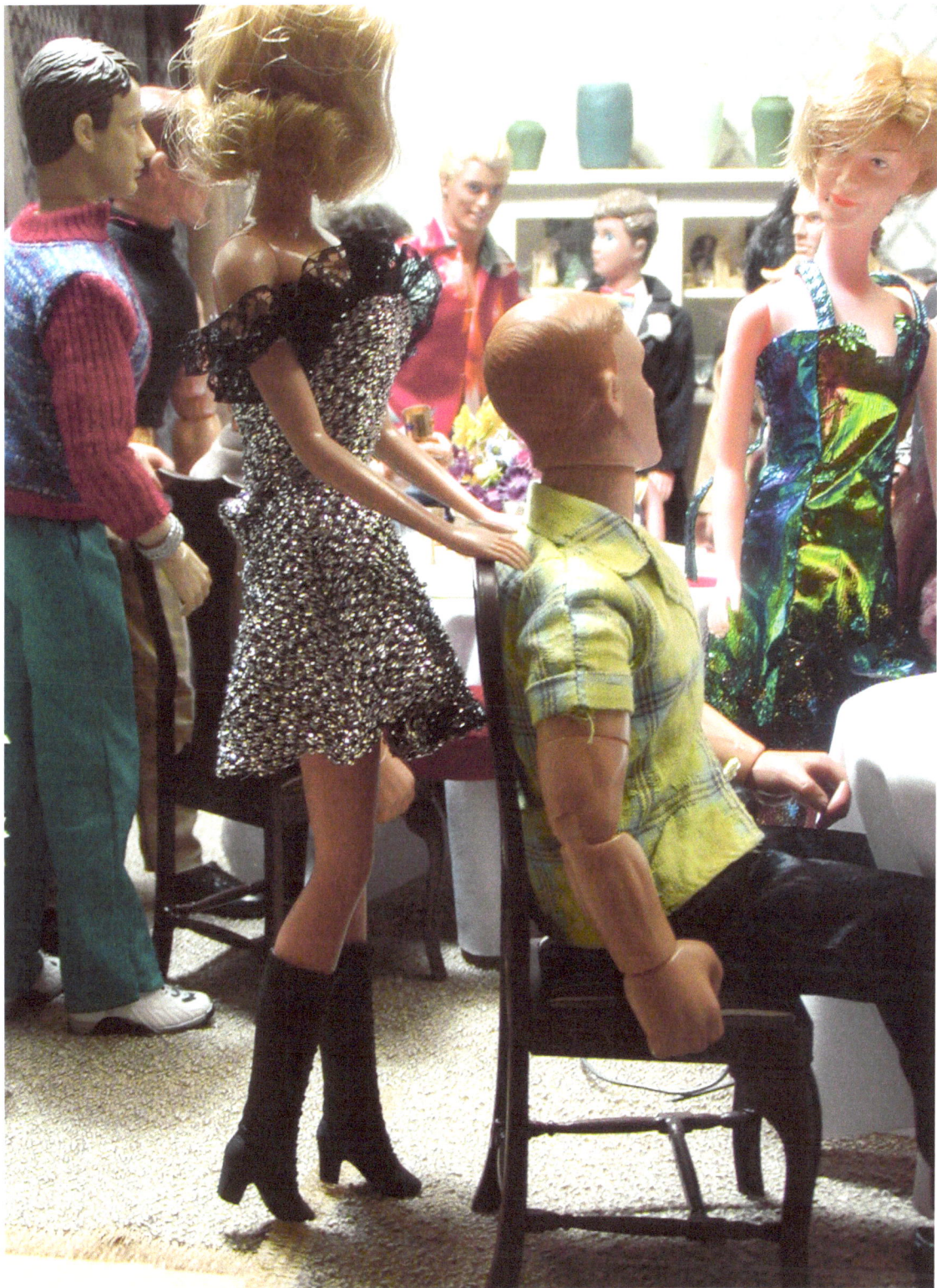

JUST WHATEVER!

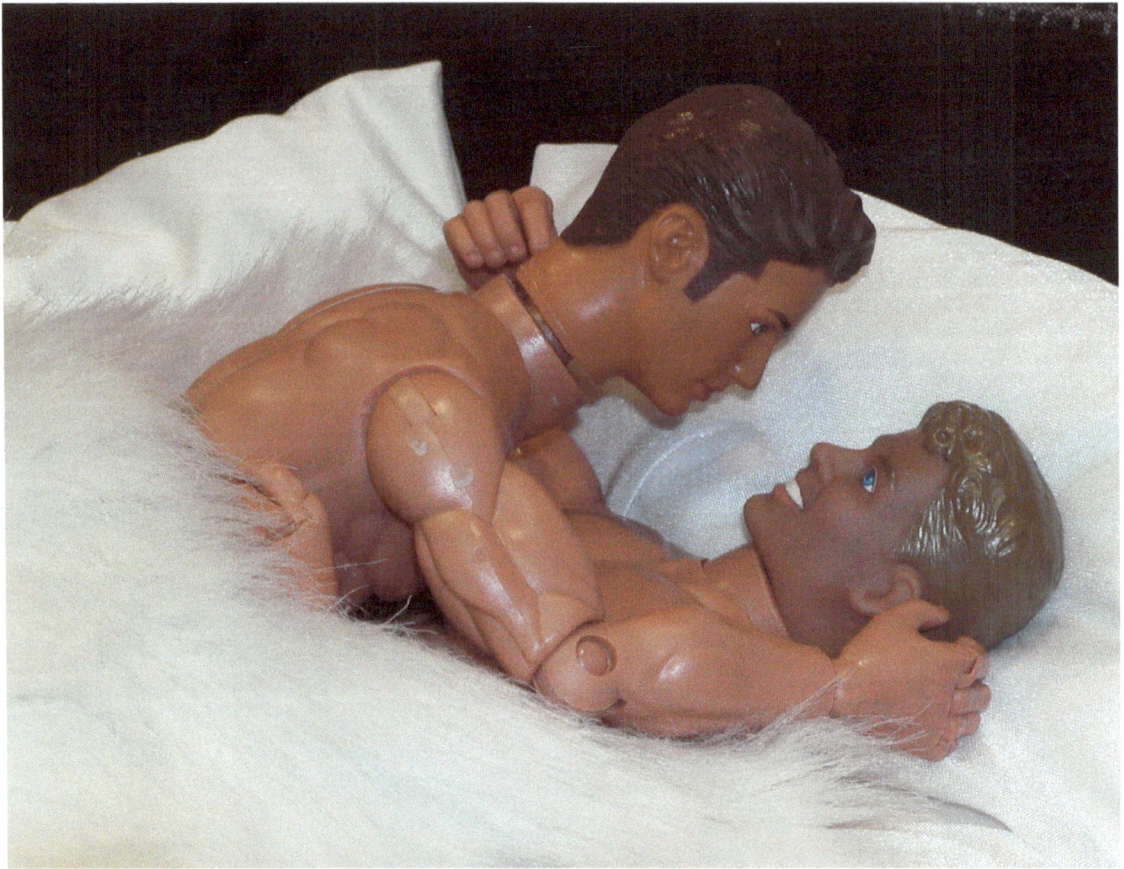

Happily Ever After